ANGOLA, CLAUSEWITZ, AND THE AMERICAN WAY OF WAR

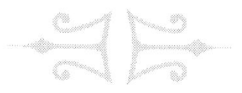

ANGOLA, CLAUSEWITZ, AND THE AMERICAN WAY OF WAR

JOHN S. MCCAIN IV

Copyright 2017 John S. McCain IV
All Rights Reserved
ISBN: 1539161056
ISBN 13: 9781539161059

The research and writing of this research paper are dedicated to my son, John, and to the men and women who fought on all sides of the conflict over Angola, Namibia, and South Africa.

*Many thanks,
LT John S. McCain IV*

TABLE OF CONTENTS

Foreword by Lieutenant General James Dubik · · · · ix
Author's Preface · xiii

Introduction: General Theory and
American Warfare · 1
What Was the South African Border War? · · · · · · · 11
Why the Angola Case Study? · · · · · · · · · · · · · · · · · 17
1976: Setting the Stage · 24
Koevoet: Police Operations on the
Angolan Border · 36
Operation Moduler: Olifants,
Ratels, and Vlamgats · 46
32 Battalion: Warfare by Different Means · · · · · · · 57
A Forgotten Conflict, a Useful Lesson · · · · · · · · · · · 64

Conclusion and Implications · · · · · · · · · · · · · · · · · 69
Appendix · 75
Chronology of Major Operations in the South
African Border War · 77
Bibliography · 81

FOREWORD BY LIEUTENANT GENERAL JAMES DUBIK

The near thirty-year South African Border War, the centerpiece of *Angola, Clausewitz, and the American Way of War*, should have been studied by security specialists years ago. Had it been, few would have been surprised by the kinds of war that followed the Cold War's end and what those wars would require. Jack McCain's book remedies this deficiency. He has applied a practicioner's eye and a professional's mind to write an interesting and important book.

The book is interesting first because of the detailed descriptions of the battles and campaigns as well as the strategy of the South African Border War. At least in the United States, this war is understudied and underappreciated.

More interesting for any national security specialist, military or civilian, is this: McCain describes an American strategic learning disability—that is, fighting wars based upon type rather than on an understanding of war—and an American misunderstanding of civil-military relationship necessary to wage war. These are significant observations.

Much of the strategic thinking in the United States follows a "war as a type" paradigm. American military and civilian strategic thinking most often understands war a spectrum—from unopposed humanitarian assistance at one extreme to full nuclear war at the other. Between are discrete points—armed humanitarian assistance, peacekeeping, peacemaking, counter terrorism, counter insurgency, limited conventional war, general conventional war, and nuclear war, to name a few. What American strategists and practicioners forget in the process is that each of these supposed-discrete points have more in common than they do difference. All are forms of war; therefore, a coherent understanding of war should preceded any discussion of "type." McCain uses this distinction skillfully to point out the errors that result from deriving strategies from type with little or no link to understanding war as a whole.

Further, McCain address the civil-military relationship necessary to wage war. He demonstrates that an understanding of the relationship between senior political and military leaders that is either based upon demonstrating who is in control of whom or upon the false belief that at the strategic level there is a hard line between policy and execution will lead a nation to folly.

Angola, Clausewitz, and the American Way of War is also an important book, for the war has much to teach. The decades-long South African Border War was a constantly changing mix of conventional, unconventional, counterinsurgey, limited war, proxy war, and clandestine operations. The senior South African political and military leaders, however, were not confused by nor overly focused on these types of war. Rather, they understood that each was a means, not an end-in-itself—a means toward achieving a political aim. Thus, they aligned both tactical battles and operational campaigns of each type with their strategic, political aim. They also aligned other military and non-military resources, policies, and actions with the political aim. They seemed to understand what some American's have forgotten: that war is an instrument of policy and that absent a strategic, political aim, tactical or operational success is meaningless. Also forgotten: that a robust and complete civil-military dialogue is necessary to achieve and sustain such alignment from a war's beginning to its end.

Jack McCain's book is not endorsement for the South African policy of apartheid, nor is it an endorsement for all of the tactics used in this war. Rather, he attempts only to shed light on this "little-known conflict" and to use it as a way to understand American strategic shortcomings. As an U.S. Army officer with over 37 years of active service myself, I can say that McCain's book is in the best tradition of American officership: he is motivated to learn and has written a book to help all of us learn with him.

James M. Dubik, PhD, is a Professor in Georgetown University's Center for Security Studies; a Senior Fellow at the Institute for the Study of War and the Institute of Land Warfare; author of *Just War Reconsidered: Strategy, Ethics, and Theory*; and retired as a lieutenant general from the U.S. Army in 2008 following his position in Baghdad as Commanding General, Multi-National Security and Transition Command, Iraq and NATO Training Mission, Iraq.

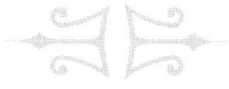

AUTHOR'S PREFACE

I originally intended this project as a way to examine the South African Border War through the context of my military experience and the study I have done through the course of my short career. I approached this document as an opportunity to truly dig into the meaning of "hybrid war" with the intent of drawing out implications for the future of warfare. "Hybrid war" is a dominant topic in contemporary military discourse and seems to be today's all-encompassing bogeyman, especially where threats to American security are concerned. Scholars, officers, and friends have seemed to become obsessed with the topic, and, therefore, I intended to make some meaning of it. This approach made sense; after all, I am a product of what

I have come to understand as "tactics and type" military: a tendency, one that I have seen firsthand, for officers to "stay in their lane" and, in doing so, to stick to where they are comfortable in terms of what tactics to use and what type of conflict to engage in.

This "tactics and type" moniker is one of my own description that I have generated as a result of my continued study into the problem, as a result of my own experiences and military socialization. Because of that process, I too had immediately assumed that the only way to classify warfare was into a separable type, somewhere on a spectrum that encompassed all possible conflict. The harder I worked and the further I dug into trying to prove that the South African Border War was indeed a hybrid war, however, the less explanatory power it maintained and the more it became apparent that I was making an all-too-common mistake and remaining in my own comfort zone. This crisis of faith forced me to reexamine every aspect of warfare I had come to understand and ultimately led me to the end result that you see before you.

Second, I need to be up front about the political connotations involved in studying this conflict in particular. In the American consciousness (and initially in mine), this war fits a convenient Western narrative, one of a racist regime bent on the oppression of nonwhites in Africa and fighting against the forces of popular national liberation. I too subscribed to this line of thinking until I began my study. As with all things generalized and many involving the African continent, the truth is far more complex and it contains much more nuance. I believe this is one of the reasons why the Border War is understudied, because of the connotations about being on the right or wrong side of history. I make no endorsement of the policy of the South African government, especially that of apartheid, and I strongly reject those that would defend apartheid, but I do believe there is value in shedding light on this little-known conflict and using it to illuminate some of my own military's shortcomings.

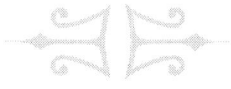

INTRODUCTION: GENERAL THEORY AND AMERICAN WARFARE

"General theory" is a well-understood term by anyone who has ever studied the discipline of political science. Bedrock concepts such as realism, liberalism, and constructivism, among others, are foundational to the study of "the art of the possible."[1] John Mearsheimer, in his seminal work, *The Tragedy of Great Power Politics*, says this about the power of general theories:

> In fact, none of us could understand the world we live in or make intelligent decisions without theories. Indeed all students and practitioners of international politics rely on theories

to comprehend their surroundings. Some are aware of it and some are not, some admit it and some do not; but there is no escaping the fact that we could not make sense of the complex world around us without simplifying theories.[2]

The relevancy of general theory is, however, challenged by contemporary political scientists such as George and Bennett in their chapter on structured, focused comparison in *Case Studies and Theory Development in the Social Sciences*. They debate the relevance of general theory, instead prompting readers to find greater explanatory power in the smaller "subclasses" of theory, which can be coined "middle-range theories."[3] The study of warfare and military operations suffers from a similar debate, although it is far more one-sided than that of political science.

In his recent book, *The Direction of War: Contemporary Strategy in Historical Perspective*, Hew Strachan attempts to articulate what he believes to be utterly lacking in modern conflict, most notably the wars in Afghanistan and Iraq: strategy. He uses the general theorist of warfare, Carl von Clausewitz, and his posthumously published magnum opus, *On War*, to guide his discussion through the legacies of the Cold War, the planning and execution of Iraq and

Afghanistan, and their meaning for contemporary strategy. He attributes the cause of this lack of true strategy to the unequal dialogue in civil-military relations. Making the point plainly, he writes,

> Waging war requires institutions which can address problems that lie along the civil-military interface, and can do so on the basis of equality rather than of military subordination to civilian control. Politicians need to listen to soldiers, to what can be done in practice as opposed to what the politicians might like to be done in theory, and to do that states need institutions within which soldiers feel ready to be realistic about the military issues—and about the nature of war.[4]

He continues on to articulate that this dysfunctional dialogue also causes the relationship between policy and strategy to be misunderstood, creating circumstances in which policy is allowed to shape strategy, but not vice versa. This document is in fundamental agreement with these points; that theory, however, does not fully capture the deficiencies in contemporary strategy.

Instead of the issue being solely within the civil-military interface, the problem is twofold, with the military being as much to blame as the civilians who control it. Not only is strategy directly undermined by the defective dialogue within the civil-military divide, but the general theory of warfare posited by Clausewitz has been supplanted by "middle-range" theories of warfare. These middle-range theories, like counterinsurgency or conventional war, lack the explanatory power of the general theory and help foster thinking that lacks strategic depth and causes the US military—and, by virtue, policy makers—to see war as something alien to its nature. Clausewitz, in his first book, made the error of this type of thinking abundantly clear: "The first, the supreme, the most far-reaching act of judgment that the statesmen and commander have to make is to establish...the kind of war on which they are embarking; neither mistaking it for, nor trying to turn it into, something alien to its nature. This is the first of all strategic questions and the most comprehensive."[5] Clausewitz completes this comment later, explaining the necessity of having thought through the war's totality before embarking on it. "No one starts a war—or rather, no one in his senses ought to do so—without first being clear in his mind what he intends to achieve by that war and how he intends to conduct it. The former is its political purpose; the latter its operational objective."[6]

These two comments are the window through which strategy should be viewed from the outset, as a totality, not part or parcel. From that beginning, the process by which middle-range theories have subsumed the general theory of warfare in US warfighting, and the negative results of that process follow in this section.

The US military has been on a constant war footing since the events of September 11, 2001. Wars have been raging in Afghanistan, Iraq, the Philippines, Africa, Syria, and other locations, in a seemingly endless trend. The discourse surrounding these conflicts centers mostly on defining what type of war we are fighting. A search of the public record shows a coherent theme in the definitions for the conflict. President George W. Bush framed it as the "Global War on Terror," a war against Islamic extremism. President Barack Obama modified that definition after taking office in a memo to the Pentagon staff and Department of Defense, stating, "This administration prefers to avoid using the term 'Long War' or 'Global War on Terror' [GWOT]. Please use 'Overseas Contingency Operation.'"[7] When conversation went from the scope of the war to its strategy, the answer almost always came instead to what type of war it was. In an attempt to redefine strategy for the Afghanistan war, the

Obama administration's main internal argument was over whether the strategy would be one of counterinsurgency or one of counterterrorism.[8] At the very highest levels, those of the commander in chief, the main point of debate had less to do with strategy and more to do with defining type and associating numbers of troops to that type. "Type" has become a replacement for "strategy" but does not hold any of its utility.

Aside from just the Obama administration's debate over Afghanistan, the US military suffers the same affliction: a fixation on type. The contemporary wars in Afghanistan and Iraq are described as wars of "counterinsurgency."[9] Russia's invasion of Ukraine is described as a "hybrid war."[10] The 1999 Kosovo War is depicted by NATO as an "Air Campaign."[11] The US Air Force does not cite its core competencies as warfighting but instead says its mission is "to fly, fight, and win in air, space, and cyberspace."[12] As a result, "strategies" for the future operations and for waging war end up being parceled into pieces, each one distinct from the other. In essence, the way the US military thinks about how it fights becomes a game of opposing forces: counterinsurgency versus conventional, naval war versus air war, special operations versus covert operations. When observing an ongoing war or a possible future war, this "type," therefore, becomes a rigid stovepipe. The result is that the war, and the strategies and policies designed to succeed in it, are mentally, doctrinally, and organizationally shaped to fit the adopted paradigm instead of adhering to Clausewitz's dictum of seeing each war for what it is and understanding war as a coherent whole. For the purposes of this document, these types are defined as the middle-range theories of warfare. By using middle-range theories as strategy, the military is beginning its decision-making process from the wrong place: from the middle.

The two issues combined—the dysfunctional civil-military dialogue and the supplanting of the general theory of warfare—make strategic decision-making within the military and by policy makers problematic. Indeed, the trinitarian nature of warfare—the relationship between the strategic, tactical, and operational levels of warfare—itself is undermined, and the balance between ends, ways, and means breaks down. The resulting confusion has been felt in all the modern wars of the United States, clearly described by Strachan: "Arguably strategy has been absent throughout the wars in Iraq and Afghanistan. In part that is because the political objects have been unclear, or variable, or defined in terms too broad to be deliverable in strategic terms. Because there has been no clear relationship between the ends and the limited (and often inappropriate) means, strategy is simply not possible."[13] He does not directly mention the tendency to utilize middle-range theories in place of the general theory of warfare, but he does mention that "counterinsurgency doctrine has only served to further complicate the relationship between the operational level of war and strategy."[14]

This confusion is deeper than simple complication; instead, it stems from the very way in which the US military views wars as separate, separable, and distinct from one another. Middle-range theories are *reflections* of the whole. They are not stand-alone, separately understandable, or distinct from war's essential nature.

Just as policy and war should be viewed as a whole, neither a form of war nor a part of war can be separated from the whole. Clausewitz makes this point clearly: "If war is a part of policy, policy will determine its character."[15] Just as with policy, middle-range theories, like counterterrorism, may inform the character of a particular war, but they operate according to the nature of war and cannot be a replacement for strategy, nor can they be decided upon a single time and left to their devices.

There must be a continuous dialogue between the soldiers and statesmen about the balance of ends, ways, and means. This requirement also generates a secondary responsibility for both the policy makers and the soldiers, one that Clausewitz thought was part of the natural assumptions of war: "It might be thought that policy could make demands on war that war could not fulfill, but that hypothesis would challenge the natural and unavoidable assumption that policy knows the instrument it means to use."[16] The realities of the United States' civil-military control apparatus compromises this assumption, giving civilians—who have little understanding of the instrument that is the US armed forces—the majority share of control. The resulting misappropriation leads to a disconnect between policy and capability, as has happened very visibly in Afghanistan. When the military views its own instruments as separate from each other, policy makers cannot be informed enough to make the right decisions, and officers start their thinking from the middle instead of the top.

The problems posed by these two seemingly systemic issues are not insurmountable, even though they seem daunting. Civilian-controlled militaries not dissimilar from our own have conducted wars similar to those of Afghanistan and Iraq in ways that maintained the balance between ends, ways, and means and had a continuous, coherent, policy-strategic dialogue that accurately reflected the realities of the war that was being fought. These same examples show militaries that didn't view the war simply from the paradigm of a middle-range theory but examined the war in a way not to make it something alien to its nature, from the general theory put forth by Clausewitz. These case studies can be highly instructive, and in examining them, lessons for how to better fight our own wars and shape our policy and strategy can be learned and assimilated. The case herein is that of South Africa during its nearly thirty-year-long Border War in Angola and Namibia. The two main thrusts of this paper are embodied in this war, making it an important case for analysis here. South Africa was fighting a war in which many different types of war were operating simultaneously. Elements of conventional, unconventional, counterinsurgency, internal civil war, and even clandestine warfare can be seen throughout the conflict in varying levels of intensity. South Africa also, despite the complicated nature of its war, did not make the mistake in conceptualizing what it was fighting and did not make an error in its dialogue.

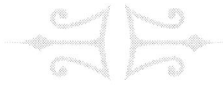

WHAT WAS THE SOUTH AFRICAN BORDER WAR?

The South African Border War is one of the least known major wars fought in modern history. It is also a conflict that is nearly wholly forgotten, in many cases intentionally, much of which is due to its association with the apartheid regime of South Africa. The fall of colonialism and the exultation regarding the myriad wars of national liberation on the continent have made objective examination difficult and fraught with associated cultural baggage. Almost no critical analysis of the conflict has been conducted outside of the few books published in South Africa and the United Kingdom, and many of those are written by former combatants reflecting on their own personal experiences. Detailed study of the Border War is also made increasingly difficult due to the competing narratives surrounding it, those of each side of the forces of the Cold War. Accounts of the battles vary greatly; for instance, the Battle of Cuito Cuanavale, discussed later, is described by some as a resounding victory for the Cuban forces, wherein they sundered the South African War effort, or, conversely as a "Vainglorious fraud [wherein the Cubans were defeated], designed to cover a retreat that had already been decided [by the Cubans]."[17, 18] These competing narratives are further complicated by the fact that South Africa's majority ruling party, the African National Congress (ANC), took part in the hostilities against the apartheid state and in the war itself, which gives veterans, many of whom were conscripts, little hope of having their war looked upon uncritically. Therefore, to shed understanding on just what the conflict was requires a significant amount of sifting and aggregation, but by doing so, the Border War—its nature and its outcome—becomes clear.

The war raged from 1966 to 1989, with combat in what is now Namibia and Angola, and with subsidiary conflict in Mozambique and South Africa proper. The major combatants were the South African Defense Force (SADF), the South West African Territorial Force (SWATF), and several Marxist-Leninist liberation fronts throughout Angola and Namibia. Levels of support for both sides were critical to their respective war efforts, and they waxed and waned with the moods and necessities of the international community and the Cold War. This support took the form of small arms and advisers and ranged all the way to new fighter jets and advanced integrated air-defense systems. The goals of both sides were in direct opposition to one another, with the South Africans trying to keep their territories and border nations from falling to pro-Communist, and therefore hostile, forces, and the Communist-backed insurgencies attempting to wrest control of their own territory from what they saw as colonial powers. In essence, the war was the same story that was played out all around the world, through the proxy wars between Cold War adversaries, but unlike the Vietnam War or even the Soviet War in Afghanistan, this conflict is nearly unknown and happily forgotten.

The war began in earnest in 1966 when South African Police, aided by elements of the South African Air Force, attacked a SWAPO base at Omugulugwombashe. This opening foray was brief and had little impact at the tactical level, but it signaled a significant shift in the South African strategy toward the escalating desire for Namibian independence. Low-intensity conflict continued as Soviet and

Chinese military advisers arrived with weapons and money, but it was not until 1975 that the war began to truly threaten the South African grip on Namibia.

November of 1974 saw the withdrawal of the Portuguese government in Angola, which created the power vacuum that would characterize the remainder of the struggle for Namibian independence and would intensify the efforts of the South Africans to exert force to regain control of the situation. In October of 1975, in Operation Savannah, South Africans advanced north across the border between Namibia and Angola to counter insurgent forces who had been conducting operations in the area known as Cuando Cubango and destabilizing Namibia. This escalation attracted the attention of both the Soviets and Cubans, who feared the loss of their toehold in southwest Africa. The Soviets pushed Castro to provide military forces, which he did by slowly flooding them into Angola.

The period between 1975 and 1987 comprised South African military incursions into the border area between Namibia and Angola, with the intensity varying until the Soviet and Cuban forces made a final push to oust the South African proxy army inside Angola, under the command of Jonas Savimbi, the National Union for the Total Independence of Angola

(UNITA). Savimbi's paramilitary group had been an unconventional warfare asset for the South Africans, and their loss would have meant the collapse of their efforts to keep Angola from becoming a Marxist-Leninist state, which would open the door for Namibia to fall the same way. To keep UNITA from collapsing, the South Africans undertook Operation Moduler, an armored assault deep into Angola aimed at dislodging Cuban and Soviet forces. Moduler, discussed later, was the last major engagement of the Border War and would help dictate the peace settlement of 1989.

Revolutionaries and professional soldiers from both sides had remarkably similar stories. Much of the combat was fought by conscripted young men fighting for what they believed was the protection of their homeland and their ideals. Some men fought with Kalashnikovs and tennis shoes, and others fought in tanks and armored personnel carriers, but regardless of platform, the fate of all Southern Africa was dependent on the final outcome of the war. Indeed, it seems that the very soul of each of the nations involved was at stake. Without oversimplifying the matter, we can say that those revolutionaries on the side of Marxism-Leninism fought for a mixture of motivations, but much of it was the cause of their own liberation. The Cubans, who arrived later in the war, fought to pay a debt to the Soviet Union and, hopefully, to expand the influence of the Cuban state. This was their first military adventure abroad and would be their only major involvement in a conflict. The South Africans fought as the Boers have since their arrival in southern Africa in 1652: like a people besieged on all sides.[19] Indeed, the ferocity of the response to the possibility of being surrounded by hostile states is distinctly in line with the Boer cultural experience, which helps explain some of their decision-making in and the prosecution of the war.[20]

This brief introduction is meant to assist in lending context to the time and geography of the conflict, but it is indeed just that, brief. The complexities of culture, politics, warfare, social upheaval, and many of the other influences that shaped the war will be addressed throughout the rest of this monograph. No one book could hope to explain in detail, however, all aspects of the South African Border War. If anything, this is an opening foray into what will hopefully be a continued critical analysis of the Border War, with the desire that it will be incorporated into the way the United States views its own capacity for waging war and making strategy.

WHY THE ANGOLA CASE STUDY?

To understand the significance of the South African Border War, and particularly the war in Angola and the border area between Namibia and Angola, it is best to start with the South Africans themselves—or, to be more exact, the Afrikaners, who made up the majority of the South African forces at the time of the Border War.

> The South African Army melded two great fighting traditions. One was that of the British Army, forged in South African participation in both World Wars. The other—arguably more significant—was that of the Boers during the Boer/South African War of 1899–1902. The

Boers held off a much larger British expeditionary force for three years, inflicting huge defeats on the British during the initial stages of the war, and being crushed eventually by a ruthless counterinsurgency campaign.[21]

This cultural experience, combined with the hardbitten life that had met the then Dutch settlers when they landed on the African continent in 1652, created a style of fighting but also a distinct mind-set about warfare that was not seen anywhere else and that contains incredible lessons for the astute observer. At no time in their history did the white South Africans fight a war in which they had the advantage, and usually they fought at a severe disadvantage. Afrikaners were noted for their brilliant tactics in their war against the British and for their utterly indomitable will to continue the fight. This process of cultural socialization is a key component in understanding how the South Africans fought the Border War and how they made decisions from the tactical level through to the strategic level.

The Border War was also the conflict that defined the role that Marxism-Leninism would have on the African continent today. While it is difficult to argue that the fundamental trajectory of history would have been altered had the forces backed by the Warsaw Pact countries won an easy victory in Namibia and Angola—some of the most resource-rich nations on earth—these events would have at the very least altered the strategic calculus of the nations that were not part of the Warsaw Pact. The importance of the African adventure to the Soviet Union cannot be understated and is evidenced by the incredible number of resources that flowed into Angola and Namibia. Fighter aircraft, main battle tanks, armored personnel carriers, integrated air-defense systems, guided missile systems, advisers, helicopters, and an immeasurable number of small arms were provided for the myriad of forces fighting the South Africans, and all of it was the most up-to-date equipment. Between 1975 and 1991, 350,000 Cuban troops served in Angola as Warsaw Pact surrogates, making it the largest combat deployment in the history of the island nation.[22] The deployments also sated Castro's desire for his particular brand of revolutionary Marxism-Leninism. Angola and Namibia were prizes to be bled for in the minds of the Soviets.

The intensity and type of combat ranged from long-range patrols—upward of one thousand kilometers on foot—conducted by teams of two South African Special Forces recces into hostile territory, to full mechanized warfare. Fighting took place on horseback and motorcycle, by parachute assault, and by *bokkie* (pickup truck), and across the borders of five nations. Logistical operations were conducted twelve hundred miles away from the South African capital city of Pretoria, eight hundred miles from the South African border, and two hundred miles into enemy-controlled territory. The South Africans never had air superiority, which meant they could not use their limited number of transport aircraft without severe risk. Therefore, movements took place across some of the harshest terrain on earth, in areas that usually did not have roads—and if they did, the roads were heavily mined. In order to overcome such tenuous lines of communication, the South Africans designed and built, while under complete embargo, an entire family of highly specialized vehicles and equipment perfectly suited for the conditions and the enemy, some of which are used by US forces today. Movements couldn't be made by road lest losses be incurred by improvised explosive devices, so instead, units would have to "bundu bash" overland through incredibly dense brush before they could engage the enemy—not to mention that this landscape was inhabited not simply by men but also by the most dangerous predators, snakes, insects, and even herbivores on the planet. The terrain, flora, and fauna were constantly trying to kill each soldier as much as the combatants were. The South Africans fought under constant air attack by MIG-23s and fought most of their battles "against enemy forces three, four, and more times their own numbers."[23] Throw in the fact that the enemy was given safe haven by the nations bordering Namibia and reinforced by large numbers of foreign troops, and the picture begins to make sense. There is no great difficulty in imagining just how hard it would be to plan and fight under conditions like these.

The difficulty alone is not what makes this case study so compelling; rather, it is what the South Africans did with that difficulty. "South African military and political leaders had a deep sense of balance and control, which stood them in good stead."[24] They assessed their situation with a clear-eyed understanding of their desired objectives and balanced their strategy to fit it, keeping in mind their tenuous position in the international community. This keen awareness of their disadvantaged international situation is unique, and it posed severe limitations on the extent of use of force. The system was not a perfect one, as the forces of fog and friction were a constant, but it was one of the most effective in modern history. Military leaders made direct efforts to find creative solutions that would assuage the strategic, operational, and tactical issues posed during the conflict, and if those solutions didn't work, they were scrapped or modified until they did. The strategic dialogue between the combatant commanders, the military leaders, and the political leaders was ever present, and at no time were the military leaders too wedded to doctrine to reconsider strategy. The leaders may have labeled the war using a middle-range theory like counterinsurgency or counterrevolution, but at no time did this inhibit them from seeing the war in its totality. Take into consideration that the enemy being fought varied from basic insurgent guerillas to an entire Cuban tank battalion, supported by a constantly shifting alliance structure based on international attention, and the sheer complexity of the war begins to unfold. This case, the South African Border War, is one that is a direct challenge to the way the United States makes strategy and views warfare today, because it is an example of it being done correctly.

Finally, this case study is utterly unknown to the American military. With great effort, sparse individual articles can be dug up, but the sheer lack of general study is shocking. There are no major books printed in the United States on the subject, and it is mentioned very rarely in any US military documents. The largest tank engagement on the African continent since the

Battle of El Alamein took place in the Border War between 1987 and 1988, which pitted a modified version of the British Challenger tank, the Olifant (elephant), against the Soviet T-62. Seemingly, there should have been at least some professional military analysis done in the West, but the most comprehensive study was done by an amateur—a lawyer from Jamaica—and only in 2013. The sheer diversity and scope of the fighting makes it a case that had the potential to help inform military decision-making about both the general theory of warfare, the middle-range theories, and the development of tactics and techniques. Much of the conflict utilized the operational doctrine of counterinsurgency, evolving many novel and counterintuitive practices that would have had direct implications for the conflicts the United States finds itself embroiled in today. Therefore, the Angolan case makes a perfect example of a war that defied conventional logic, defied simple definition, and deserves the attention of historians, political scientists, and military scholars. Robert Goldrich sums up this point best in this quote from *The Best Defense*: "The tactical and operational lessons from the Border War mostly variations on usual military themes—solid and relevant training, doctrine, and attitudes—but the most significant lessons of this conflict for the United States are far broader, and sobering in nature."[25]

1976: SETTING THE STAGE

The South African Border War started in earnest on August 28, 1966. The conflict had its roots in the popular liberation struggles that had been springing up in numerous African nations. From about 1960 onward, a tidal wave of national liberation swept across southern Africa and elsewhere in the world. Infant nations like Botswana, Congo, Kenya, and others were beginning to assert their influence and aid like-minded aspiring liberators. The Warsaw Pact saw these rolling conflicts as an opportunity to spread the message of Marxism-Leninism, which would expand the Soviet sphere of influence and allow them a foothold in resource-rich areas. Western nations were less expansionist in their views but saw the necessity to keep the dominos from falling and to leverage anticommunism into a spread of democracy. Most importantly to the Border War, Zambia had achieved its independence from Britain in 1964, which would prove a major complicating factor for the South African Defense Forces (SADF). A major flash point for the war was the manner in which South West Africa (Namibia) was administered by South Africa: "Officially Namibia was administered 'in the spirit' of the old League of Nations mandate of 1919 (which was revoked by the International Court of Justice in 1971), but in practice it was simply run as a fifth province of the [South African] Republic."[26] This de facto colonial control by South Africa created a useful root cause with which Marxist-Leninist insurgents could begin driving a wedge between the people of Namibia and agitating for popular revolution, and "free Namibia" became a rallying cry of SWAPO and other groups. This colonialism also helped ingratiate revolutionaries to the international community, due to the fervent anticolonial sentiment in Western nations.

The South Africans practiced the policy of apartheid in what they knew as South West Africa, now Namibia, and tensions were set to boiling when "in 1959 a public protest in Windhoek's Old Location against a forced population removal to Katutura led to a police shooting and the death of 11 people, while 54 were wounded."[27] With the pressures of the national liberation movements, unrest, and the territorial control of Namibia, the stage was set.

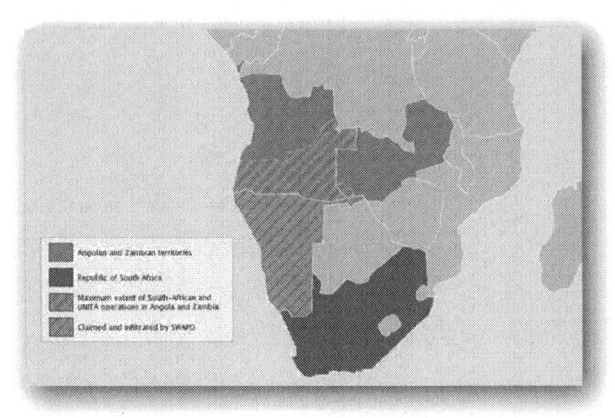

The outgrowth of the anger among the people of Namibia materialized in the form of the South West Africa People's Organization, known as SWAPO, founded April 19, 1960. SWAPO adhered to the doctrinal teachings of Marxism-Leninism, which is one of the reasons why they incurred so much of the wrath of the South Africans. As the movement grew, they began to militarize, sending officers to be trained abroad in places like Cuba and the Soviet Union in order to learn guerilla tactics and strategy, increasing their capabilities and their following. Eventually, when they began organizing full-fledged military bases, they began to pose a major threat to South West Africa. "The war is generally thought to have started on 28 August, 1966, when a force of 130 men—mostly policemen under the command of commandant (Lieutenant-Colonel) Jan Breytenbach and 9 of his paratroopers from 1 Para Bn—swooped down on the secret SWAPO base of Ongulumbashe in Ovambo with 35 Alouette III helicopters."[28]

Neither SWAPO nor the South Africans had much technical proficiency. The fighting was brief but intense,[29] and "after having been decimated at Ongulumbashe, SWAPO did not enter Ovamboland again for some years. Instead, the Caprivi Strip, being relatively accessible from Zambia, for the time being became the main battleground."[30] The South Africans forced SWAPO into hiding in Zambia, but they were alienated from their traditional support base, which was in Ovamboland, not the Caprivi Strip, denying the enemy a "centre of gravity."[31] The group was alive and able to operate and refit, but it was isolated and unable to project force for the time being.

While the war in Namibia was put on the back burner by the South Africans, events half a world away would entirely shatter the strategic situation in favor of SWAPO. On April 24, 1974, a coup d'etat swept away the Fascist Portuguese military dictatorship. The new regime had little inclination to continue spilling blood and treasure into the endless hole that was their African Empire, and they announced the withdrawal of Portuguese forces from Mozambique, Guinea-Bissau, and Angola. According to the South Africans, "This changed everything."[32] SWAPO leader Sam Nujoma wrote in his memoirs, "Our geographical isolation was over. It was as if a locked door had suddenly swung open. I realized instantly that the struggle was in a new phase...For us [it] meant that...we could at last make direct attacks across our northern frontier and send in our forces and weapons on a large scale."[33]

Besides the fact that SWAPO was now allowed to operate out of a borderland of Namibia and back into Ovamboland, a key component to a successful insurgency, they gained a new ideologically aligned ally: the People's Movement for the Liberation of Angola, or MPLA. The power vacuum left by the rapid exit of the Portuguese created a scramble for dominance, sprouting several different movements, including the MPLA. The MPLA had the firm backing of the Cubans and the USSR; they were fully resourced with conventional weapons and began to fight fiercely against the other two pro-Western groups, the National Liberation Front of Angola (FNLA) and the National Union for the Total Independence of Angola (UNITA).

"Within a few weeks, MPLA forces drove FNLA out of Luanda, after which UNITA, which had no more than a token presence in the capital, withdrew to the South."[34] The massive escalation now presented a much more serious threat to South Africa and especially to Namibia; however, Prime Minister John Vorster was hesitant to get more involved militarily. "He relented only when the governments of the United States (US), Zambia, Zaire, and Liberia implored him to move in and stop the Marxist advance from taking power in Luanda."[35]

The solution became what is known as Operation Savannah. The strategic aim was to "employ a limited war to apply pressure to the OAU [Organization of African Unity] so they'd put in place a government of national unity."[36] The operation consisted of four phases: "Aid to the anti-Marxist movements in Angola with regard to battle training, logistics, and intelligence. Preventing any further advance of the enemy. Recapture of all areas occupied by the MPLA and Cubans in their Southward march. The capture of southern Angolan harbours."[37] Commanded by Jan Breytenbach, the lightning advance of South African troops caught the Cubans and MPLA by surprise, shattering their forces. This tactical victory turned into a strategic defeat, however, when it was roundly condemned by the international community, which resulted in the loss of support for South Africa by the United States and began a strategic narrative that would shape the way South Africa fought for the remainder of the war.

The strategy of South Africa had been, until this point, one of a strategic defensive. The South Africans went on the offensive only in order to limit the capability of SWAPO and the MPLA to threaten South West Africa. Their military involvement had been limited to only two major actions between 1966 and 1975. After 1975, the war began to unravel for the SADF, and they were forced to leave Angola in 1976, giving SWAPO and the MPLA freedom to attack into South West Africa at will. SWAPO set up bases within sight of the Namibian border again, back in Ovamboland and out of Caprivi, and the loss of face for South Africa proved a boon to SWAPO recruiting. "According to South African intelligence, SWAPO's military strength increased from about 400 trained guerillas in 1974 to approximately 2,000 in 1976."[38] The soldiers who had been fighting until now were conscripts from South Africa. They did not know the bush and had little investment in the situation save for their military duties: "[Successive efforts] infiltrated into northern Ovamboland in the wake of South

Africa's retreat from Angola. They caught exactly nothing in their nets...Battalions of infantry moved backward and forward through the bush in long sweep lines...It was the biggest deployment of South African troops since World War II, and this huge force didn't get a single kill."[39]

Yet SWAPO continued to gain ground and influence. A total arms embargo of South Africa was looming. The strategy wasn't working, and South Africa was beginning to lose the war. They needed a new mind-set and a new way of fighting to forge a new way forward, which came in the form of General Jannie Geldenhuys and Prime Minister Vorster's new strategic initiative.

Both the statesman and the soldier looked at the war they were fighting and did not make it something alien to its nature. In 1977, South Africa enabled the Namibians to choose their own political structure, removed apartheid laws from the books, and, most importantly, legitimized SWAPO as a permitted political party, a seemingly counterintuitive move.[40, 41] Geldenhuys understood the highly political nature of the war, and indeed, he applied a label of "revolutionary war," but by this he did not commit himself simply to low-intensity (read: middle-range) doctrine or principles.[42] Both the prime minister and Geldenhuys instead took a holistic view of what would be needed to prosecute the war successfully. The strategic dialogue went as follows: the chief of the SADF was given the political objectives by the prime minister. Next, both Geldenhuys and Magnus Milan (first as chief of the SADF and then as defense minister) would present options shaped by the political and strategic considerations and confer with the State Security Council (SSC) to refine the approach. Finally, the prime minister would approve or work with SSC and the generals to make changes, and the process would start all over again as the strategic picture evolved.[43]

The overall strategy decided upon was to inhibit Namibia from becoming another Marxist-Leninist state or a threat to South African security and to "win enough time to create conditions in which SWAPO would lose an election."[44] He had clear objectives: establishing a political situation in which an independent Namibia could hold democratic elections and preventing violence from being used as a means to seize power in Namibia. He assessed what capabilities the SADF had, what limitations they had, and where the SADF could be improved to make it more effective tactically and operationally. The international situation was taken into account, ultimately resulting in the realization that South Africa was alone in its fight.

In order to tackle the embargo, new military acquisitions took priority to modernize the SADF and allow it to operate in the unique terrain and conditions in which it would be fighting. The SADF identified their acquisitions needs, generated a requirement, and oversaw the development of the individual weapons systems. Parliament was informed about the development progress and approved funding.

In order to carry out the new strategy, Geldenhuys needed experts on the ground who knew the culture and had a personal investment in the stability of Namibia, but at the same time, the regime needed to maintain its support from the South African people.

> In the military field, the changes were reflected in an ever increasing number of blacks fighting for the South African administration, 32 Bn (consisting of ex FNLA fighters) being the first unit to allow blacks to join…This was followed by the 31 Bn (Bushmen), 101 Bn (Ovambos), 201 Bn (East Caprivi), 202 Bn (Okavango), 203 Bn (West Caprivi), and 911 Bn (ethnically mixed). Especially 32 and 101 Bn were much more than ordinary infantry battalions, growing into what amounted to motorized infantry brigades. Many blacks also joined the Police

COIN unit Koevoet. With the exception of 32 Bn (SADF) and Koevoet (SAP), these all became part of the South West Africa Territorial Force (SWATF), an indigenous Namibian force under South African command that, during the eighties, supplied about 70 percent of the military manpower in the territory, about 30,000 men. More than 90 percent of these had black, yellow, or brown skins.[45]

This was a monumental change to the South African forces, one that allowed the precarious political situation, maintaining support by the South African people, to be balanced.[46] It also gave Namibia a force of people who had a personal interest in seeing the fight come out in their favor and who lent unparalleled expertise regarding the local area and culture.

Geldenhuys also took an incremental goal-setting strategy with his commanders. "[The commanders'] mission would be revised periodically; when the set goal had been achieved, the parameters would be scaled up. In this way realistic goals were set...in due course it became a realistic mission for them to completely clear their respective areas of all insurgents."[47] This goal-setting process was one internal to the SADF, but it fit the overall strategy as decided by the civil-military dialogue. A hearts-and-minds operational plan was put into place, as was a potent counterinsurgency operational doctrine. This process continued through the relationship of Geldenhuys and Vorster. Their relationship created an environment in which they both looked at the war as a whole, assigned objectives, created a strategy, and maintained a constant balancing of ends, ways, and means. There was an equal civil-military dialogue, and there was no middle-range-theory paralysis.[48]

In order to examine how the process looked and worked in practice during the Border War and to elicit meaning that can be applied to the US military, three different types of warfare will be examined. Each one can be described with the label of a middle-range theory, but they do not truly conform to the US conception of such. The three to be examined are Koevoet operations (COIN), conventional operations, and a third category that defies easy description, 32 Battalion operations. There were more types of operations being conducted, such as special operations, but the three herein provide the best examples for the purposes of this document. When considering the fact that all of these types were conducted simultaneously, it becomes apparent that the war was looked at as a whole and was not made something alien to its nature.

KOEVOET: POLICE OPERATIONS ON THE ANGOLAN BORDER

The word *koevoet* literally means "crowbar" in Afrikaans. It was the brainchild of Johannes Dreyer, a South African police brigadier general, after he learned from the Rhodesian experience. "I learned in Rhodesia that you must use the local population because of their knowledge of the customs, terrain, and language. An all-white force would be really ineffective in this kind of war."[49] The intention was to create a unit whose sole purpose was to literally "pry" the insurgents away from the local population. After the failures of the massive sweep raids in 1976 and 1977, it was obvious that something new had to be tried, and the ultimate result was the Koevoet force. Officially titled South West African Police Counterinsurgency (SWAPOL COIN), the unit was a highly controversial, if novel, take on a way to wage a counterinsurgency. The unit did not utilize soldiers but instead used experienced police officers, either from the South African police or the South West African police, as combat leaders. Police were used for several reasons. First, police officers had investigative skills that normal soldiers lacked. They were more adept at questioning witnesses, finding evidence, and reading people, and therefore they were highly suited to the task of tracking down insurgents in an open landscape such as that of northern Namibia. Second, police were not drawn from the military, and therefore, if they were killed, it was less likely to cause an uproar at home in South Africa. This had a second-order effect of reinforcing the narrative that this war was a civil war, not an insurgency. The policemen were all volunteers and had been subject to a grueling selection course under "as realistic conditions as possible."[50] By the time they had completed the selection course and were operational, they were more akin to paramilitary officers with a police background than they were to normal police officers.

Along with the police, "of [Koevoet's] operational personnel, 90 percent were black, most of them locally recruited Ovambos."[51] Many of the black soldiers were recruited from villages in the surrounding area, which gave them a keen insight into the local mood. It also gave them an investment in the local area, as the insurgents were within many of the villages they were from. These special police were able to exploit local intelligence that would never have been available to SADF forces unless they had individual soldiers who stayed in the area over long periods of time. Koevoet also recruited from former SWAPO insurgents, as one Koevoet officer remarked in 1986: "They're paid reasonably well, given uniforms, fed; any service-related injuries are treated by our doctors or medics. The conditions are one thousand percent better than what they ever had with SWAPO. Hell, I guess we have forty or fifty ex-terrs [short for "terrorist," a colloquialism used to describe insurgent fighters] in Koevoet right now, and not one has ever deserted and run back to SWAPO."[52]

Koevoet tactics were as simple as they were effective. A convoy of four mine-resistant ambush-protected vehicles with about forty black special constables and four white officers would leave a base camp that had been set up in the local area. The vehicles, usually Casspir armored vehicles, were extremely heavily armed, usually with multiple heavy machine guns, and every police officer had as much ammunition as could be carried, further solidifying them as much more akin to paramilitary forces than police. The tops of the vehicles were also specially modified so they were open, allowing all occupants to stand and fire outward or take cover as necessary. The idea was "maximum firepower...you can have too little but you can't ever have too much."[53]

Each convoy was assigned a specific patrol box near the Angolan border. They would then proceed to a local village, known as a *kraal*, and question the inhabitants or head to an area where SWAPO had been rumored to be and search for spoor. *Spoor* is an Afrikaans word for signs of animal activity such as prints, broken grass or branches, or anything else that might indicate the presence of quarry. Once spoor was found, the proverbial chase was on. Teams of Ovambo trackers would run ahead and give chase: "Cars flanking them, the black policemen moved at a dead run, often outstripping the APCs, which couldn't keep pace through the thick brush. They would go until winded, drop back to the Casspirs, and their places would be taken by others who jumped off the sides of the rolling cars and took the tracks."[54] This interesting tactic was adopted from the same way South Africans hunt game, using trackers ahead to help in chasing the animal with the hunter following closely behind; therefore, it was a familiar pattern to all parties. While a notable example, it was not the only cultural tool that the South Africans relied on in the war.

Once the spoor was fresh enough to consider the enemy close by, the trackers would return to the vehicle, and all guns would be pointed outward. Hot pursuit, where Koevoet members would follow insurgents into Angola if they had good spoor, and often if they didn't, was an allowed practice. This was a violation of international law—crossing into another sovereign nation—but South Africa relied on the degree of opacity surrounding the border area to bolster the practice. This was an important tactic because it kept SWAPO insurgents from digging in just across the border for easy hit-and-run attacks, and thereby complicating SWAPO's operational picture and limiting their offensive options. The vehicles would continue in the direction of the last known movement of the enemy and engage them once it was possible. Overwhelming firepower was used to subdue whatever insurgents were unlucky enough to be found. Teams were also motivated to track down insurgents by highly controversial bounties offered for captured equipment or for killed insurgents.[55] The possibility of extra cash encouraged risk taking but also increased the level of brutality of Koevoet and incentivized killing instead of taking prisoners, a morally questionable activity, to say the least. Teams would spend one week in the bush and one week at base, maintaining that operational tempo for months on end. Ultimately, Koevoet teams killed 3,323 insurgents during the years they operated on the Angolan border, making their kill ratio 1:25.[56]

This form of relentless counterinsurgency had significant tactical-level effects, some positive and some negative.[57] Being an insurgent became a highly unhealthy profession in the areas that Koevoet was responsible for. The enemy was kept under constant pressure and wasn't allowed to get comfortable even if the insurgent was inside Angolan borders, thanks to the lax interpretation of the hot-pursuit rule. The idea was to literally pry out insurgents from the local population, and Koevoet indeed did so. Through their relentless tracking, engaging, and keeping SWAPO on the back foot, SWAPO was unable to operate freely. By using locals as police constables, Koevoet ensured that there was expertise and a cultural tie with the Ovambo people, who were the main target of SWAPO. In essence, Koevoet denied SWAPO easy access to the local center of gravity, the population of Ovamboland itself. This direct pressure from Koevoet forced SWAPO to take harsher measures to maintain what control they had with the Ovambos. Measures included killing local chiefs suspected of cooperating, coercing young men and women to become fighters, and compelling subsistence support from villages. Koevoet was also inexpensive to run compared to a similar army unit. The logistical support necessary was minimal, and they operated relatively autonomously.

Koevoet, however, utilized brutal methods to combat insurgents. Accounts of atrocities are not difficult to find, and the Truth and Reconciliation Commission in South Africa took the stance that Koevoet operators committed crimes against humanity and that the bounty system utilized to motivate operators created an environment in which abuses and excesses were prevalent.[58] Did they tactically help or hurt? Perhaps the best quote that sums up the tactical-level ambiguity comes from the firsthand account of an American journalist in *Beneath the Visiting Moon,* when he asked about local support for SWAPO:

> Around here, which is where you find the heaviest infiltration, a lot of them are pro-SWAPO. The further you go west or east, the less support you find. There are certain [villages] we know where the [local populations] help them, but there are others that are definitely anti-SWAPO. That's where we get most of our info from the local [population]. They may not like us, but a lot of them like the terrs even less.[59]

The operational-level effect of Koevoet operations had much to do with their ability to keep the enemy from making anything permanent. They were small, fairly independent units that operated in isolation from SADF forces, but they punched well above their weight. Koevoet denied the enemy the capability to set the conditions for either tactical or strategic success and bled them of resources and men, which further complicated their operational picture. In essence, Koevoet disabled insurgents from any true purchase in the battlespace.

At the strategic level, Koevoet operations were more of a success than at the tactical level. Support for SWAPO in the area did not significantly grow while Koevoet was stood up. Koevoet also limited the time in which insurgents could have contact with the population, undermining their influence. They kept SWAPO from infiltrating farther south than Ovamboland, which supported the overall strategy of keeping Namibia from becoming a Marxist-Leninist state. Koevoet also bought time and space, a strategic goal of South Africa, to allow the democratic process to begin to take shape, and it did so at little cost to the overall South African force in men and resources. Finally, Koevoet forces bled SWAPO of men and much-needed equipment—a tactical and operational victory but one with the strategic effect of making support expensive to Cuba and the USSR. Koevoet was just one piece in a very large strategic picture.

Koevoet was indicative of the flexible thinking that the SADF and the South African government were capable of in this conflict. While Koevoet officers were police officers and labeled a COIN force, they were very much more than that, and COIN doctrine did not limit their tactical or operational flexibility. In fact, they were unlike anything that had come before. The unit very much made its own rules, but in doing so, it was not beholden to a "type." They just did what was effective. Koevoet was also an example of the properly functioning civil-military dialogue. The insurgency problem had been well identified, along with the political ramifications. Both the generals and the statesmen knew that outward escalation into the border area would inflame international opinion, and military casualities would cause heartache at home. However, the military needed an effective method of blunting the SWAPO offensive. The solution that materialized, Koevoet, was exactly the right one: a blend of political and military needs driving an innovative way forward.

ANGOLA, CLAUSEWITZ, AND THE...

Casspir Mk3 Armored Personnel Carrier[60]

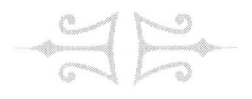

OPERATION MODULER: OLIFANTS, RATELS, AND VLAMGATS

As 1986 was coming to a close, the strategic situation in Angola was shifting.[61] After the 1984 Lusaka accords, South Africa had been forced to pull all military forces out of Angola.[62] International pressure against the South Africans had increased, even after compliance, creating a situation ripe for SWAPO. SWAPO poured fighters into southern Angola and northern Namibia in an attempt to win control of the area. South Africa's ally, UNITA, had been doing its part by denying SWAPO fighters access to the Caprivi Strip and the area known as Kavango, but they were weakened after years of fighting. Their weakening or defeat would also complicate matters in South Africa proper:

"If UNITA were neutralized, it would make it easier for [African National Congress] fighters to infiltrate South Africa from their camps in Angola via Botswana."[63] The situation grew worse when, in January 1987, a massive Soviet airlift brought heavy armor, BMP-1 IFVs, and heavy weapons, in upward of ten flights per day.[64] The Communists also brought massive air support with them. "MIG-21s, -23s, and SU-22s were deployed at Menonque. They stationed a helicopter force, consisting of Mi-8s, Mi-17s, Mi-25s, and Mi-35s at Cuito Cuanavale."[65] Advanced air defenses were emplaced at the airfields, and the moving convoys had organic man-portable and fixed air defenses.[66] South Africa knew that in order to retain control of the situation, they would have to launch a major offensive into Angola or lose UNITA and probably the entire war.

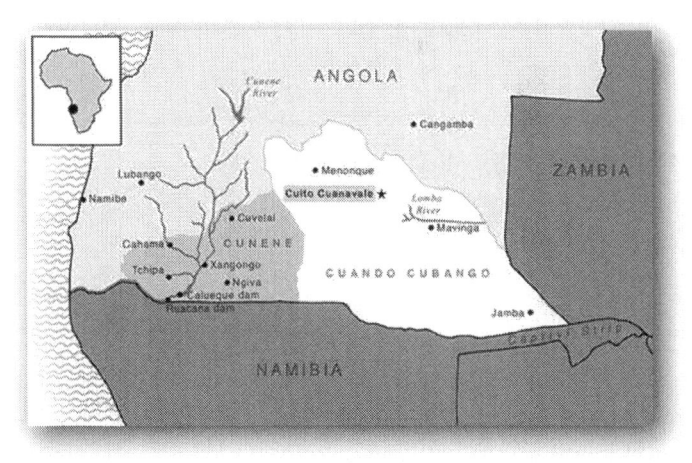

The stage for a massive conventional battle was set at a confluence of two rivers, the Cuito and Cuanavale, at an airstrip where the mechanized forces of Soviets, Cubans, and FAPLA were massing for their assault on UNITA. The force constituted the center of gravity for all of Angola where South Africa was concerned. FAPLA and Cuban forces began to advance on UNITA forces, who were ill equipped to take on heavy armor. South African special forces were deployed to support UNITA with antitank weapons but could not get into range to attack.[67] A second plan took shape, to use troops from the 32 Battalion to delay or possibly halt the advance of the FAPLA and Cuban tank column.[68] South Africa was still extremely worried about the international situation and was reluctant to use a force that was not plausibly deniable. The embargo and sanctions had taken a toll on South Africa. The 32 Battalion was reinforced by the South African Sixty-First Mechanized Battalion Group, without their tanks and G-5 155-millimeter artillery, but only as a defensive measure.

FAPLA continued its advance on UNITA, and the measures that the South Africans were taking to try to stop them were ineffective. Something else had to be done, lest the war be entirely lost. "On August 28, General Geldenhuys, Lindenberg, and the Chief of the Air Force Lieutenant General Denis Earp visited Rundu.

There they saw that even the artillery reinforcements wouldn't be enough and finally decided to lift all restrictions on the use of 61 Mech (minus the tank squadron) and the SAAF."[69] This huge increase in involvement in Angola meant that South Africa could no longer deny its role there, dramatically changing the strategic situation.[70]

By the time the battle was imminent, the Cuban-FAPLA forces consisted of about six thousand men and eighty tanks, plus artillery and air support from Mig-21/23s. The South African force of the 32 Battalion and Sixty-First Mechanized amounted to about fifteen hundred men and 120 Ratel infantry fighting vehicles (IFVs). The South Africans did not have air superiority, heavy armor, or adequate air defenses, leaving them open to attack from the air and the ground. However, rapid mechanized forces were a modern version of the old mounted cavalry of the Boer War in the minds of the South African forces. This type of warfare was well suited to the cultural tendencies of the Afrikaners, and they proved especially adept at it in this case.

While almost impossible to give a punch for punch without dedicating an entire book to the subject, over the course of the next several months, a mechanized tête-à-tête took place between FAPLA and Cuban forces and those of UNITA and South Africa. The fighting was fierce, nothing like the low-intensity counterinsurgency simmer that had been going on near the border with Namibia. The South Africans, despite not having armor, used massed Ratel-90 IFVs equipped with 90-millimeter cannons and high-explosive antitank (HEAT) rounds. One on one, they were no match for the T-55, but as a mobile and organized formation, they inflicted withering casualties on the Warsaw Pact tanks. What ensued was the largest mechanized fight on the African continent since El Alamein. The Cuban-FAPLA offensive was slowed in successive engagements but not entirely blunted until October 3, 1987.

The Forty-Seventh Brigade, the main Cuban-FAPLA armored formation, moved toward the Lomba River in an attempt to break out from the South African forces that had pinned them down. The South Africans took this as an opportunity to inflict a knockout blow on the enemy and rapidly organized a joint attack with UNITA and the Sixty-First Mechanized at daybreak of October 3. The book *Battle on the Lomba* gives a harrowing story of an individual Ratel-90 crew and their attack on a group of T-55 Main Battle Tanks of the Forty-Seventh Brigade. What comes through is the reliance on maneuver to close the distance between armored formations and the use of rapid fire to hit the tanks in between their own shots. A single 100-millimeter projectile from a T-55 would "slice a Ratel open like a [steel] knife through a bully beef tin lid."[71] The battle was a lopsided victory for the Sixty-First Mechanized: "FAPLA's 47 Brigade was basically wiped out, with more than 600 men killed and dozens of tanks and armored vehicles taken out. The SADF losses, on the other hand, were incredibly light, only one soldier killed... and one Ratel destroyed."[72] The end result was not a knockout blow, and the fighting continued for more than a month after, until the end of November. Despite the best efforts of the Sixty-First Mechanized and the stunning victory at Lomba, the FAPLA force was not completely destroyed. They were able to retreat out of the reach of the South Africans and were still a threat until the eventual peace agreement in 1989. The war continued to escalate, eventually bringing large numbers of conventional forces to bear, but at best it can be described as a stalemate, with the SADF trying to inflict as much damage as possible on Castro's forces and Castro trying to save face by searching for a victory before his eventual pullout from Angola.

At the tactical level, the South African Sixty-First Mechanized had just blunted the largest armored offensive ever seen in western Africa, and it did so without any tanks, while severely outnumbered and outgunned. The SADF used fighting traditions from its past to develop new tactics and techniques to take on weapons systems that it had absolutely no business fighting.

Their performance at Lomba was stunning, but once the enemy was on the retreat, it became nearly impossible to pin them down again. They were able to regroup and were a threat for the remainder of the war. Despite the victories, tactically, Operation Moduler was a draw.

At the operational level, the shift from a counterinsurgency operational doctrine to one of fast-moving mechanized warfare was made rapidly. There was little debate on what needed to be done, with the primary consideration being minimizing the footprint so as not to ignite international fury. The SADF denied FAPLA and the Cubans freedom of movement, inflicted huge costs in men and matériel, and complicated support from the Soviet Union and Castro. The cost to the SADF was relatively low as well; they lost thirty-one men and five Ratel IFVs.[73] But the enemy was never decisively defeated and was still able to move its forces at will within Angola.

Strategically, the South Africans accomplished the goal they set out to accomplish. UNITA remained an ally and was not overrun by FAPLA, allowing South Africa to deny Caprivi and Kavango to SWAPO. This constituted a major escalation of the war for South Africa, however, and resulted in staunch international condemnation. The worsening international situation made life significantly more difficult for the South Africans, which resulted in further isolation. This had an interesting, if unexpected, effect on the strategic calculus of the South Africans. "With the growing cult of isolation, it no longer became necessary for Pretoria to maintain 'deniability' in its actions in southeast Angola."[74] This isolation emboldened Prime Minister P. W. Botha, inciting in him "greater recklessness."[75] Strategically, Moduler was both a victory and a loss for South Africa.

When faced with an almost systemic shift from a "COIN" war to a "conventional" war, the South Africans did not need to make sweeping changes to their forces. The strategic picture was merely taken into account, and the war continued to progress, maintaining the same political objectives as in the beginning of the war. There was no debate about type, and, in fact, many of the same units that had already been fighting on the border continued to do so under new conditions. The general theory of warfare was what mattered to the South Africans in this case, even though the focus was different. The civil-military dialogue was concise, and the consequences were understood by both policy makers and generals. Both parties knew the political and military ramifications of the major escalation, and as a result, the Sixty-First Mechanized had been authorized for use by P. W. Botha at the discretion of Geldenhuys. The decision-making process is further indicative of the properly functioning civil-military dialogue in South Africa at the time.

Oryx Helicopter[76]

Alouette III Helicopter[77]

ANGOLA, CLAUSEWITZ, AND THE...

Ratel ZT3 A2 Antitank Missile System[78]

Olifant Mk2 B Main Battle Tank with 105-mm Gun[79]

GV6 MK 1: Gun-Howitzer, Medium, Self-propelled; 155-mm[80]

R4 Assault Rifle[81]

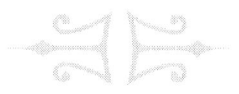

32 BATTALION: WARFARE BY DIFFERENT MEANS

Throughout the Border War, there was a single unit that was involved in just about every major operation and effort, a unit that defies the label of a middle-range theory: 32 Battalion. As much myth as truth surrounds their existence and operations. They were part conventional, as they were armored at points in their history and used as regular infantry. They were part unconventional in that they conducted raids across the borders of Angola, disguised as FAPLA or SWAPO soldiers to harass, undermine, and kill. They were a part-mercenary force, as they used Portuguese-speaking former insurgents as unit troops. They were meant to "out-guerilla the SWAPO guerrillas."[82] In doing so they would "get them [SWAPO] off balance and keep them on the wrong foot until they began to collapse psychologically and subsequently also militarily."[83] The "Terrible Ones" were the most effective and most controversial unit in the history of the SADF.

Founded by the controversial, the "eternal Colonel" Jan Breytenbach, the unit had inauspicious beginnings that are a study in the complexity of the situation in Angola.[84] The first recruits were from the National Front for the Liberation of Angola (FNLA). They were one of the alphabet soup of liberation groups in Angola, which were actually in direct combat with the later critical ally of South Africa, UNITA. During Operation Savannah in 1975, under the command of Breytenbach, his FNLA and separate UNITA troops fought against Cubans and FAPLA in a bid to take the capital city of Luanda. The operation failed and is described in the memoirs of Breytenbach: "Operation Savannah was a brilliant operation in most tactical respects, but strategically it failed miserably. This was due solely to the crumbling resolve of the South African politicians, particularly Prime Minister John Vorster, toward the end of the campaign."[85]

Breytenbach may have overstated the "crumbling resolve," but it was during this period that the tide of the war turned sharply against South Africa.

After the abortive Savannah, Breytenbach went on to officially form the 32 Battalion around the core of former FNLA troops, commanded by hand-selected white officers from the infantry, special forces, and paratroopers.[86] The unit then transformed into the quasi-guerilla force that operated entirely inside Angolan borders, inflicting incredible and constant damage on SWAPO. The 32 Battalion would engage SWAPO insurgents whenever and wherever possible, and they did so while wearing enemy camouflage, using captured AK-47s, and eating captured enemy rations, all of which only added to the element of fear and confusion. Breytenbach describes the results:

> The guerrilla war developed into a battle of wits between 32 Battalion platoon leaders and SWAPO detachment commanders…No matter how hard they tried, SWAPO never found a way to combat the havoc caused by our platoons. They tried to move in larger bodies for greater protection, but this only presented us with bigger targets. They even tried to counterattack on horseback, which certainly took us by surprise.[87]

When SWAPO resorted to battalion-sized formations, the 32 Battalion used semiconventional methods to attack them in force. All of this was done while they were based inside enemy lines with almost no access to resupply save for a single Unimog truck every two weeks.

A striking example of their sheer combat prowess took place at the Battle of Savate. In May of 1980, the 32 Battalion was tasked with attacking the FAPLA-held town of Savate. UNITA intelligence had estimated that there were three hundred FAPLA troops in the city and passed that intelligence to SADF forces, along with a request to use the 32 Battalion to attack the garrison. The 32 Battalion dispatched three understrength companies with a mortar section, totaling fewer than 250 men, to mount the attack.[88] Most of the men from the 32 Battalion were armed with small arms and hand grenades. What took place was extraordinarily heavy fighting, due to the fact that instead of the expected three hundred enemy soldiers, there were 1,066 hardened FAPLA fighters armed with heavy machine guns, rocket launchers, and other heavy weapons. Eventually, the entire FAPLA brigade was routed by the Buffalo Soldiers, and they beat a hasty retreat away from Savate.[89][90] This victory robbed FAPLA of a base of operations that had been used to attack south into Namibia, allowing UNITA to occupy it, thereby strengthening the overall position of South Africa.

As time went on, the power and reputation of the Buffalo Soldiers grew. Their mix of unconventional techniques and conventional attack capability, as well as fearlessness, made them the go-to force for the South Africans when the going got rough. During the 1987 battle of Cuito Cuanavale, the 32 Battalion was employed as a conventional element in the armored assault northward into Angola, even before the Sixty-First Mechanized was. Seemingly, there was very little that the soldiers of the 32 Battalion couldn't do. They continued to be the most effective unit of any in the entire Border War in terms of enemies killed. The 32 Battalion remains one of the most notorious units of the conflict. They were ultimately dissolved shortly after the end of the Border War in 1993. Their legacy as a quasi-mercenary force and their almost mythical status played against them, as they became a political hot potato in the forming of the new, postapartheid South African government.[91]

The tactical successes of the Terrible Ones are well documented.[92] Their fearless guerilla-style pursuit of the enemy inside their lines may have been their hallmark, but it was much more their adaptability that held so much utility for the SADF. Their ability to move from covert raids to fully mechanized warfare defies the conventional logic of middle-range theories.

They also contributed to the tactical success of the majority of the operations conducted on or north of the Namibian border because of their intelligence-gathering capabilities and their intimate familiarity with insurgents in their area.

Operationally, the 32 Battalion helped set the conditions for strategic success through enabling other units to operate freely along the Angolan border. They also provided tactical support for UNITA, which allowed pressure on the SADF by SWAPO to be relieved in the Caprivi Strip and Kavango. Resupply was also limited, forcing them to equip with captured enemy equipment, making them nearly cost-free for the SADF, save for pay. The utter terror that the Buffalo Soldiers instilled in the enemy and their commanders also made the enemy forces more cautious in their efforts to cross the border, forcing them to take a slower operational tempo and denying them space to maneuver or mass forces.

At the strategic level, the 32 Battalion punched well above their weight in terms of effects. Such a small unit shaping an entire battlespace is almost unheard of. The breathing space they created for UNITA, for the regular forces of the SADF, and even for the Koevoet helped maintain political support in South Africa proper. A majority of the fighters were former FNLA, and if they were killed in action, their names were not showing up in the newspapers. They were a deniable unit, helping to quell the international situation while still being incredibly effective in killing the enemy. They operated in a strategic gray space and became the on-call unit for any situation that necessitated their huge array of skills. The 32 Battalion was more than a win-win for South Africa; they helped shape the strategic situation in the country's favor. They are also an example of an outfit that does not fit neatly into any definition, and there is nothing analogous in contemporary conflict. Strategically, the 32 Battalion was a huge success. The Terrible Ones kept the political cost of the war low in a time when it needed to stay that way, their ambiguous nature was deniable, and the majority of the casualties were not South Africans.

The 32 Battalion was an unconventional unit, but they did not fit neatly into that label. Soldiers from the Buffalo Battalion fought using everything from knives to infantry-fighting vehicles and were the go-to force when things got tough, and at no point did they believe themselves incapable of a task because it was not their area of expertise. They moved through all types of warfare without difficulty. The unit was also a useful civil-military solution to the complicated political necessities of the war. The soldiers were mostly Angolan, and their actions were highly effective but did not incur further political cost due to escalation.

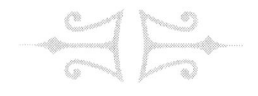

A FORGOTTEN CONFLICT, A USEFUL LESSON

The South African Border War finally came to an official close on December 22, 1988, when the Tripartite Accord was signed by South Africa, Cuba, and Angola. The agreement set out the conditions under which all parties were to exit Angola and stipulated that democratic elections would be held in Namibia. The combat had engulfed all of southern Africa, and it is important to note that it was not just confined to the border between Namibia and Angola—the war took many forms. "The South Africans were fighting a conventional war in Angola, a counterinsurgency war in Namibia, an unconventional war in Mozambique, and localized civil disturbances within

South Africa."[93] The fighting consisted of much more than just the three types examined in this document, those of Koevoet operations, of mechanized assault, and of the 32 Battalion. The South Africans did not see the war through the lens of separate parts, however, nor were any types fought in isolation; all were fought at the same time. These types are instructive because throughout the conflict they evolved as the strategic situation did. The war was labeled a "counterrevolutionary" war when the conflict broke out, but instead of tying itself to a single operational doctrine, the relationships among ends, ways, and means adapted as the character of the war did.

The overall strategic goal was to keep Namibia from becoming a Marxist-Leninist state and therefore a grave threat to the security of South Africa. This goal was at the forefront of the minds of the three prime ministers who prosecuted the war: John Vorster, P. W. Botha, and F. W. De Klerk. The generals whose goal it was to help shape strategy and fit it to operational and tactical means did so with severe constraints, mostly emanating from the declining international situation. A continuous and highly effective strategic dialogue took place between the policy makers and soldiers throughout the years of the war to work within those constraints and within the constraints of embargo and tenuous at-home political support. The result is described in the *South African Journal of Military Studies*: "SWAPO failed in spreading their war wide. Their attempts to activate Caprivi, Kavango, and the Kaokoveld—let alone the rest of the country—bore no fruit. On the contrary, the SADFs avowed goal to limit the insurgency to Ovamboland was a resounding success."[94] SWAPO, in the end, came to power through the democratic elections process, but this was not what they had intended. Instead they had fought for a non-democratic Marxist-Leninist state. South Africa had prevented SWAPO from achieving its stated political goal: unfettered power.

Whether the South African generals read Clausewitz is unknown, albeit highly likely, but they held to his teachings as the war unfolded. They considered the political objective of the war, understood the war's context on influencing those political goals, and combined civilian and military means to reach that goal, never considering the military means in isolation from their purpose.[95] They understood the need to maintain political legitimacy, as well as possible, at home and in the eyes of the international community, going so far as to use creative means to do so, like the 32 Battalion. Policy also never made demands of the war that it could not fulfill. South Africa did not attempt to reshape the political character of Namibia; on the contrary, they tried only to keep it from becoming Marxist-Leninist, something that it was not at the time of the war. They kept an insurgency at bay and a conventional offensive at bay, all while maintaining that one policy goal. Most importantly, South Africa did not allow doctrine or middle-range theories to inhibit their ability to see the war as it was. As a result, there was never an attempt to make the war something alien to its nature, and when the character of the war changed, the South Africans adapted to it. There was no protest when armor was used in what was until then a counterinsurgency war. No new training was required for SADF forces; all that changed was the equipment.

The South African war effort was far from a perfect one. Mistakes were absolutely made throughout the war. For instance, due to the worry about international pressure, the SADF refused to bring armor to the front at Cuito Cuanavale, despite the presence of T-55s. Had the forces of luck been against the SADF, the battle could have been a potential massacre. The war was fought as a defensive war, and the offensive was taken only as a way to blunt the will of the enemy and deny it the ability to maneuver or expand, not to destroy it. This defensive strategy limited the objectives of the war to make them achievable, but it also allowed SWAPO to remain vital. Despite the tactical and operational victories and the lack of a strategic loss—the end result was more of a draw than a victory—the South African regime of apartheid was doomed to failure. The political goal of the conflict itself was achievable, but the policy of a domestic political regime that subjugated one race of people in favor of another was impossible to maintain. The purpose of the regime was so out of alignment with the realities of the contemporary international system that it was utterly impossible for any government in Pretoria to be considered legitimate. There is no legitimacy possible when a government robs its citizens of basic human dignity. The Border War was well fought, but the regime behind it undermined any true success that could have been attained. It is no surprise that the system of apartheid fell just over a year after the end of the war.

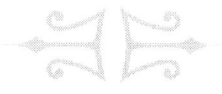

CONCLUSION AND IMPLICATIONS

The South African case is an instructive one for military leaders and policy makers to pay particular attention to, as it has implications that can be useful in determining our own ability to see, shape, and wage war. First and most importantly, as Clausewitz stated in *On War*, we must look at war as a whole, neither making it something alien to its nature nor trying to see it strictly from one of the limited paradigms of type. Type can be useful! Type can lend analogy or help to begin to determine the capabilities necessary for a conflict. Type can even be a good starting point to help shape tactics and operations. However, in the American practice—and not in the South African experience—type became much more than a tool;

it became the frame for the wars themselves. Words like "counterinsurgency strategy" (President Obama's own words) should make every strategist, soldier, and policy maker shudder. A strategy may incorporate elements of counterinsurgency in its operational design, but strategy is so much more.

Strategy must account for all aspects of a nation if it is to be successful. Economic power, public support, diplomatic considerations, and acquisitions are just some of the basic components that should be involved in strategy, because strategy goes beyond just fighting. Even in so-called limited wars, failing to account for all the moving pieces when making strategy is a recipe for disaster.[96] There is no simple or quick war, regardless of how it may be sold or what political commentators may say; nor is war a science. While far reaching, the basics of the Clausewitzian general theory of warfare are imperative to the success of the state in the conduct of a war. Attempting to supplant a middle-range theory in place of a true strategy violates the general theory. South Africa had this right in its wars; the United States does not in ours.

Along with recognizing and understanding the right aperture through which to approach strategy, those charged with making strategy must realign the civil-military dialogue. An exchange like that in Robert

Gates's *Duty*, in which the president tells his civilian and military leaders, "I am giving an order," is indicative of just how poor the civil-military dialogue is.[97] Both *Duty* and *Obama's Wars* paint a dire picture of the decision-making process and how the United States goes about making war. Military leaders are mostly looked to for one-time input, in the case of the Afghanistan surge, for a desired number of troops. There was severe distrust on the part of the Obama administration as to the true intention of the military, relegating them to the role of adversary. Military leaders were not only disempowered but had to sell their strategy instead of have a conversation about it. Political consideration, while important, trumped sound strategy making. There was even worry of empowering General Petraeus too much, for fear that he would be a potential contender in the next presidential race. The fact that this was allowed to affect the strategy of a major war shows the level of discord; however, it is not unique to the Obama administration, as the Bush administration had a similar politically driven decision-making process under Rumsfeld.[98, 99]

Hew Strachan concludes that the civil-military in its ideal involves "the democratic head of state [setting] out his or her policy, and the armed forces [coordinating] the means to enable this achievement." And therefore, "the reality that is [strategy] is iterative, a dialogue where ends also reflect means, and where the result—also called strategy—is a compromise between the ends of policy and the military means available to implement it."[100] American political and military leaders need to incorporate this understanding into the process of decision-making for both going to war, waging wars, and concluding them. Civilian control of the military does not denote a one-way process in which military leaders lend opinions on occasion. The dialogue should be constant and continually reflect the changing realities of the war itself and the home front. Most importantly, policy—and by its virtue, strategy—must be attached to the possible.

What is also made abundantly clear in the South African example and its contemporary American counterpart is that *the integrity of the strategic decision-making process between the civilian leaders and the military leaders is of paramount importance.* To wage a war correctly requires more than a civilian leader simply giving policy marching orders to the military. However, the military also cannot simply remain comfortable hiding behind apoliticalism. Leaving politics to the politicians relegates military decision-making to purely military considerations, which is only a single aspect of war. Strategic decision-making is a two-way street, and whereas politicians have no problem making military decisions, military leaders have been eager to stay in their military lane. Military leaders should rightly avoid *partisan* politics but not politics entirely, and statesmen should do more than take occasional, unequal advice from military leaders. Regardless of the size or scope, war is an all-encompassing phenomenon that requires constant reevaluation. Both civilian and military leaders would do well to recognize that fact.

While a full critique of the Afghan and Iraqi Wars is outside the scope of this document, their legacy should be considered carefully as a lesson in the breakdown of the civil-military dialogue and the misuse of middle-range theories as strategy. The South African Border War presents a useful counterexample for consideration, but in order to be successful in future wars, it is the United States that must change. War, regardless of scale, is the all-encompassing national act of force and effort "to compel [your] enemy to do [your] will."[101] An enemy should be expected to make every effort to undermine, disrupt, and ruin your strategic plans, requiring constant reassessment at every level, and whereas the military may physically do the fighting, it is the state that decides to go to war, wages the war, and finishes it. Neither policy makers nor any member of the US military should forget either fact.

APPENDIX

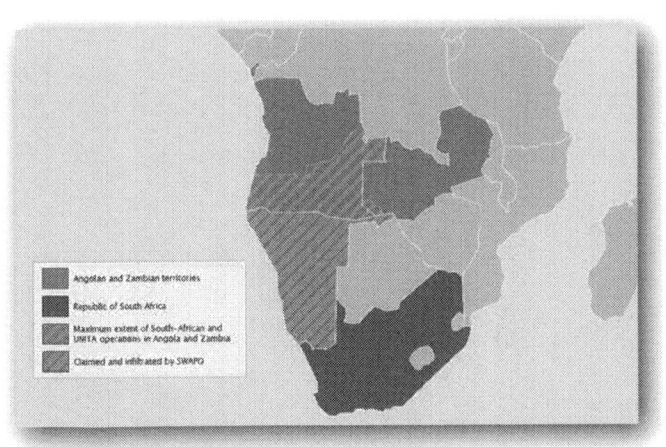

A map illustrating the extent of the different territories and who controlled them during the South African Border War[102]

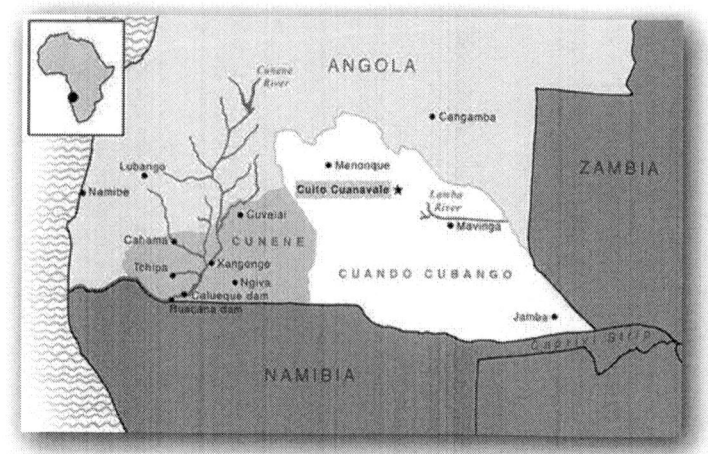

A view of the operational area of the Border War[103]

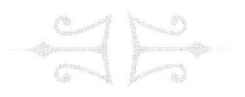

CHRONOLOGY OF MAJOR OPERATIONS IN THE SOUTH AFRICAN BORDER WAR

Attack on Ongulumbashe (August 1966)—South African Police and South African Air Force attack on SWAPO elements in Ovamboland

Operation Savannah (October 1975–March 1976)—South African conventional forces attack into Angola to disrupt SWAPO operations

Operation Reindeer (May 1978)—Airborne "vertical envelopment" attack on a SWAPO operational base at Cassinga

Operation Rekstok (March 1979)—South African cross-border attacks on SWAPO bases inside Angola in conjunction with Operation Saffraan

Operation Safraan (March 1979)—South African cross-border attacks into Zambia to attack SWAPO elements that had retaliated for operation Reindeer by rocketing the Caprivi Strip town of Katima

Operation Sceptic (June 1980)—A large mechanized infantry assault into Angola on SWAPO and PLAN bases at Chifufua, Ionde, Mulola, and Chitumba, as well as a follow-on sweep for SWAPO insurgents

Operation Klipklop (July 1980)—Helicopter assault by South African troops on the town of Ruacana to destroy a PLAN logistics base

Operation Protea (August–September 1981)—Mechanized assault into Angola intended to neutralize SWAPO military forces in Angola between the Cuene and Kavango Rivers (the largest operation of the war)

Operation Makro (December 1981–January 1982)—A military attempt to create a no-man's-land for SWAPO and FAPLA in southern Angola

Operation Meebos 1 (March 1982)—With the same aim as Operation Makro, Two Parachute Battalion was attacked by a large FAPLA force. A counterattack was made by 61 Mech, puching FAPLA back.

Operation Meebos 2 (July–August 1982)—Sweep operations against FAPLA and SWAPO by 32 Battalion, First Parachute Battalion, and Sixty-First Mechanized Battalion

Operation Askari (December 1983–January 1984)—A large-scale mechanized assault into Angola in order to destroy SWAPO logistics and command and control capabilities to disrupt a SWAPO incursion into Namibia

Operation Phoenix (April 1983)—A retaliatory attack on SWAPO elements that had been attacking civilian farms in Namibia

Operation Alpha Centauri (August 1986)—An attack on the airfield at Cuito Cuanavale by UNITA, supported by the 32 Battalion and SADF 155-mm G-5 Howitzers

Operation Moduler (August–November 1987)—This was a mechanized assault into Angola to inhibit Cuban and FAPLA forces from destroying UNITA. This particular series of running battles saw SADF Ratel IFV's take on Cuban T-54/55 tanks.

Operation Hooper (January–February 1988)—A mechanized assault by the South Africans in order to pursue the surviving FAPLA units from Operation Moduler across the Cuito River, therefore securing UNITA forces from annihilation

Operation Packer (March–April 1988)—A continuation of Operation Hooper to push surviving Cuban and FAPLA troops across the Cuito River to ensure they were no longer a threat to UNITA

BIBLIOGRAPHY

"The Arrival of Jan Van Riebeeck in the Cape—6 April 1652." South African History Online. Accessed March 28, 2012. http://www.sahistory.org.za/topic/arrival-jan-van-riebeeck-cape-6-april-1652.

Breytenbach, Jan. *The Buffalo Soldiers*. Alberton, South Africa: Galago Publishing, 1999.

Campbell, Horace. "The Military Defeat of the South Africans in Angola." *Monthly Review*, April 2013.

Clausewitz, Carl Von, Michael Howard, and Peter Paret. *On War*. Princeton, NJ: Princeton University Press, 1976.

Crocker, Chester A. *High Noon in Southern Africa: Making Peace in a Rough Neighborhood*. New York: W. W. Norton, 1992.

Donnelly, Thomas. "Rumsfeld's War." *Weekly Standard*. December 15, 2004. http://www.weeklystandard.com/rumsfelds-war/article/6246.

Gates, Robert Michael. *Duty: Memoirs of a Secretary at War*. New York: Knopf Doubleday Publishing, 2014.

Geldenhuys, Jannie. *At the Front: A General's Account of South Africa's Border War*. Jeppestown, South Africa: Jonathan Ball, 2009.

George, Alexander, and Andrew Bennett. *Case Studies and Theory Development in the Social Sciences*. Cambridge, MA: MIT Press, 2005.

Goldrich, Robert. "Annals of Wars We Don't Know About: The South African Border War of 1966–1989." *Foreign Policy*. March 12, 2015. Accessed January 1, 2016. http://foreignpolicy.com/2015/03/12/annals-of-wars-we-dont-know-about-the-south-african-border-war-of-1966-1989/.

Heitman, H.-R. *South African Armed Forces*. Cape Town, South Africa: Buffalo Publications, 1990.

Hooper, Jim. *Beneath the Visiting Moon: Images of Combat in Southern Africa*. Lexington, MA: Lexington Books, 1990.

Ignatius, David. "The Problem with America's Limited Wars." *Washington Post*. October 9, 2014. Accessed March 05, 2016. https://www.washingtonpost.com/opinions/david-ignatius-reality-check-on-limited-war/2014/10/09/19c8c95e-4ff2-11e4-babe-e91da079cb8a_story.html.

Jones, Seth. "US Efforts in Afghanistan Will Fail If Taliban Not Routed from Pakistan." Counterinsurgency in Afghanistan: RAND Counterinsurgency Study. 2008. Accessed March 1, 2016. http://www.rand.org/pubs/monographs/MG595.html.

"The Kosovo Air Campaign (Archived)." NATO. October 13, 2015. Accessed March 02, 2016. http://www.nato.int/cps/en/natohq/topics_49602.htm.

Lord, Dick. *From Fledgling to Eagle: The South African Air Force during the Border War*. Johannesburg, South Africa: 30 Degrees South, 2008.

Mannall, David R. *Battle on the Lomba, 1987: The Day a South African Armoured Battalion Shattered Angola's Last Mechanized Offensive; A Crew Commander's Account*. Solihull, UK: Helion and Company, 2015.

Mearsheimer, John J. *The Tragedy of Great Power Politics*. New York: Norton, 2001.

Nortje, Piet. *The Battle of Savate: 32 Battalion's Greatest Operation*. Cape Town, South Africa: Zebra Press, 2015.

Nujoma, Sam. *Where Others Wavered: The Autobiography of Sam Nujoma*. London: Panaf Books, 2001.

Polack, Peter. *The Last Hot Battle of the Cold War: South Africa vs. Cuba in the Angolan Civil War*. Oxford, UK: Casemate Publishers, 2013.

Pottinger, Brian. *The Imperial Presidency: P. W. Botha; The First Ten Years*. Johannesburg, South Africa: Southern Book Publishers, 1988.

Saunders, Paul. "Why America Can't Stop Russia's Hybrid Warfare." *National Interest*. June 23, 2015. Accessed March 2, 2016. http://nationalinterest.org/feature/why-america-cant-stop-russias-hybrid-warfare-13166.

Scholtz, Leopold. "The Namibian Border War: An Appraisal of the South African Strategy." *Scientia*

Militaria: South African Journal of Military Studies 34, no. 1 (2006): 19–48. doi:10.5787/34-1-15.

Scholtz, Leopold. *The SADF in the Border War, 1966–1989*. Cape Town, South Africa: Tafelberg, 2013.

Steenkamp, Willem, and Helmoed-Romer Heitman. *Mobility Conquers: The Story of Sixty-One Mechanized Battalion Group, 1978–2005*. Solihull, UK: Helion and Company, 2016.

Stiff, Peter. *The Silent War: South African Recce Operations, 1969–1994*. Alberton, South Africa: Galago Publishing, 1999.

Strachan, Hew. *The Direction of War: Contemporary Strategy in Historical Perspective*. Cambridge, UK: Cambridge University Press, 2013.

Truth and Reconciliation Commission of South Africa Report. Cape Town, South Africa: Truth and Reconciliation Commission, 1999.

US Air Force—Mission. "US Air Force—Mission." Accessed March 2, 2016. https://www.airforce.com/mission.

Wilson, Scott, and Al Kamen. "'Global War on Terror' Is Given New Name." *Washington Post*. March 25, 2009. Accessed March 10, 2016. http://www.washingtonpost.com/wp-dyn/content/article/2009/03/24/AR2009032402818.html.

Woodward, Bob. *Obama's Wars*. New York: Simon and Schuster, 2010.

1. This quote is attributed to Otto Von Bismarck, describing politics.

2. John J. Mearsheimer, *The Tragedy of Great Power Politics* (New York: Norton, 2001), 8–9.

3. Alexander George and Andrew Bennett, *Case Studies and Theory Development in the Social Sciences* (Cambridge, MA: MIT Press, 2005), 266.

4. Hew Strachan. *The Direction of War: Contemporary Strategy in Historical Perspective* (Cambridge, UK: Cambridge University Press, 2013), 24.

5. Carl von Clausewitz, Michael Howard, and Peter Paret. *On War* (Princeton, NJ: Princeton University Press, 1976), 88–89.

6. Ibid., 579.

7. Scott Wilson and Al Kamen, "'Global War on Terror' Is Given New Name," *Washington Post.* March 25, 2009. Accessed March 10, 2016. http://www.washingtonpost.com/wp-dyn/content/article/2009/03/24/AR2009032402818.html.

8. Bob Woodward, *Obama's Wars* (New York: Simon and Schuster, 2010).

9. Seth Jones, "US Efforts in Afghanistan Will Fail If Taliban Not Routed from Pakistan," *Counterinsurgency in Afghanistan: RAND Counterinsurgency Study* 4. 2008. Accessed March 1, 2016. http://www.rand.org/pubs/monographs/MG595.html.

10. Paul Saunders, "Why America Can't Stop Russia's Hybrid Warfare," *National Interest*, June 23, 2015. Accessed March 2, 2016. http://nationalinterest.org/feature/why-america-cant-stop-russias-hybrid-warfare-13166.

11. "The Kosovo Air Campaign (Archived)." NATO, October 13, 2015. Accessed March 2, 2016. http://www.nato.int/cps/en/natohq/topics_49602.htm.

12. US Air Force, "US Air Force—Mission." Accessed March 2, 2016. https://www.airforce.com/mission.

13. Strachan, *The Direction of War*, 218.

14. Ibid.

15. Clausewitz, *On War*, 606.

16. Ibid., 607.

17. Horace Campbell, "The Military Defeat of the South Africans in Angola," *Monthly Review*, April 2013.

18. Willem Steenkamp and Helmoed-Romer Heitman, *Mobility Conquers: The Story of 61 Mechanized Battalion Group, 1978–2005* (Solihull, UK: Helion and Company, 2016), 1038.

19. "The Arrival of Jan Van Riebeeck in the Cape, 6 April 1652," South African History Online, March 28, 2012, http://www.sahistory.org.za/topic/arrival-jan-van-riebeeck-cape-6-april-1652.

20. Since their arrival at the South African Cape, the Boers have been beset by just about every hostile force that was able to reach them. This siege mentality can be seen throughout their cultural history and was exacerbated by the two Boer Wars fought against the English. The Boers were offered a "free state" by the British and settled there until gold and diamonds were

discovered in the territory. The British resultantly attempted to reincorporate the Orange Free State by force.

21. Robert Goldrich, "Annals of Wars We Don't Know About: The South African Border War of 1966–1989." *Foreign Policy*, March 12, 2015. Accessed January 1, 2016. http://foreignpolicy.com/2015/03/12/annals-of-wars-we-dont-know-about-the-south-african-border-war-of-1966-1989/.

22. Ibid.

23. Ibid.

24. Ibid.

25. Ibid.

26. Leopold Scholtz, "The Namibian Border War: An Appraisal of the South African Strategy," *Scientia Militaria: South African Journal of Military Studies* 34, no. 1 (2006), 19–48. doi:10.5787/34-1-15.

27. Ibid.

28. Ibid.

29. Peter Stiff, *The Silent War: South African Recce Operations, 1969–1994* (Alberton, South Africa: Galago Publishing, 1999), 36–37.

30. Leopold Scholtz, *The SADF in the Border War, 1966–1989* (Cape Town, South Africa: Tafelberg, 2013), 10–11.

31. Ibid., 11.

32. Ibid., 12.

33. Sam Nujoma, *Where Others Wavered: The Autobiography of Sam Nujoma* (London: Panaf Books, 2001), 228–29.

34. Scholtz, *SADF in the Border War*, 16.

35. Ibid., 14.

36. Ibid., 18.

37. Ibid., 17–18.

38. H. R. Heitman, *South African Armed Forces* (Cape Town, South Africa: Buffalo Publications, 1990), 146; Scholtz, *The Namibian Border War*, 29.

39. Jan Breytenbach, *The Buffalo Soldiers* (Alberton, South Africa: Galago Publishing, 1999), 149.

40. Scholtz, *The Namibian Border War*, 32.

41. After its political legitimization, SWAPO relied more on its armed wing, the People's Liberation Army of Namibia (PLAN), to conduct combat operations. I continue to use "SWAPO," as the distinction is unnecessary for the clarity of this document.

42. Jannie Geldenhuys, *At the Front: A General's Account of South Africa's Border War* (Jeppestown, South Africa: Jonathan Ball, 2009), 87.

43. This process is best seen in the 1979 SSC meeting, where then chief of the SADF, Milan, presented the "forward" and "close" defense options to the SSC and P. W. Botha. This is indicative of the type of strategic dialogue taking place within the SADF and the South African government at the time.

44. Scholtz, *The Namibian Border War*, 33.

45. Geldenhuys, *At the Front*, 77.

46. Scholtz, *The SADF in the Border War*, 51. This was first identified as a needed change in a top-secret assessment by the South African National Intelligence Service. With that direction, the services generated the necessary policy.

47. Ibid., 90.

48. This point is reinforced by Geldenhuys's memoir, *At the Front*.

49. Jim Hooper, *Beneath the Visiting Moon: Images of Combat in Southern Africa* (Lexington, MA: Lexington Books, 1990), 108.

50. Ibid., 107.

51. Ibid., 43.

52. Ibid., 106.

53. Ibid., 50.

54. Ibid., 61.

55. *Truth and Reconciliation Commission of South Africa Report* (Cape Town, South Africa: Truth and Reconciliation Commission, 1999), 43, 62, 75.

56. Ibid., 77.

57. It is very difficult to ascertain exactly what happened on the border under the Koevoet operations umbrella; in fact, it is one of the least well-documented parts of the war effort. Both sides of the conflict were noted for using propaganda to its fullest potential. SWAPO played up abuses by Koevoet (and invented some) in order to inflame international opinion against the South Africans as oppressors—a highly useful tactic at the time, which aided their strategic position. Koevoet tried to frame its operations as being for the good of the locals and that they were liberating them from the evils of a Marxist-Leninist revolution that murdered local leaders and committed excesses in order to maintain control and instill fear. As with most counterinsurgency conflicts, it is difficult to get a feel for exactly what went on day to day. There is only one source on Koevoet

operations on the Angolan border from an impartial (as much as possible) source, the book *Beneath the Visiting Moon*. The book is a firsthand account of operations with Koevoet in 1986 and 1987 from the perspective of an American journalist. I use this book as a source but do not necessarily believe it is entirely comprehensive. To get primary source material would be outside the scope of this document and would require an entire project on its own.

58. *Truth and Reconciliation*, 77.

59. Hooper, *Beneath the Visiting Moon*, 54.

60. Photo credit: South African Army.

61. *Vlamgat* is literally translated from Afrikaans to mean "flaming hole." In colloquial usage it was used to refer to the Mirage F1 fighter aircraft.

62. Chester A. Crocker, *High Noon in Southern Africa: Making Peace in a Rough Neighborhood* (New York: W. W. Norton, 1992), 195.

63. Scholtz, *The SADF in the Border War*, 254.

64. Ibid., 252.

65. Dick Lord, *From Fledgling to Eagle: The South African Air Force during the Border War* (Johannesburg: 30 Degrees South, 2008), 394.

66. Ibid., 394.

67. Scholtz, *The SADF in the Border War*, 259.

68. Ibid.

69. Ibid., 261–62.

70. It is not clear whether the prime minister was informed prior, but given the previous civil-military relationship, it stands to reason that he was well aware and agreed before the plan moved forward.

71. David R. Mannall, *Battle on the Lomba, 1987: The Day a South African Armoured Battalion Shattered Angola's Last Mechanized Offensive; A Crew Commander's Account* (Solihull, UK: Helion and Company, 2015), 205.

72. Scholtz, *The SADF in the Border War*, 276.

73. Geldenhuys, *At the Front*, 240.

74. Brian Pottinger, *The Imperial Presidency: P. W. Botha, the First Ten Years* (Johannesburg, South Africa: Southern Book Publishers, 1988), 377.

75. Ibid.

76. Photo credit: South African Air Force.

77. Photo credit: South African Air Force.

78. Photo credit: South African Army.

79. Photo credit: South African Army.

80. Photo credit: South African Army.

81. Photo credit: South African Army.

82. Breytenbach, *The Buffalo Soldiers*, 178.

83. Ibid.

84. Breytenbach was promoted to colonel in 1977. His expertise and ability merited promotion to general officer, but his lack of patience for staff officers and rear-echelon officers, as well as his characteristic bluntness, kept him at colonel until his retirement in 1987. He had first joined the SADF in 1950.

85. Breytenbach, *The Buffalo Soldiers,* 123.

86. Ibid., 140.

87. Ibid., 191.

88. Piet Nortje, *The Battle of Savate: 32 Battalion's Greatest Operation* (Cape Town, South Africa: Zebra Press, 2015), 67.

89. The term "Buffalo Soldiers" was the informal nickname for the unit. The unit insignia was the head of a cape buffalo with crossed arrows behind it, invoking the impression of strength with the cape buffalo and bellicosity with the arrows.

90. Buffalo Soldiers was a common usage nickname for 32 Battalion.

91. Breytenbach, *The Buffalo Soldiers*, 340.

92. The Terrible Ones is a common usage nickname for 32 Battalion.

93. Peter Polack, *The Last Hot Battle of the Cold War: South Africa vs. Cuba in the Angolan Civil War* (Oxford, UK: Casemate Publishers, 2013), 170.

94. Scholtz, *The Namibian Border War*, 47.

95. Clausewitz, *On War*, 87.

96. David Ignatius, "The Problem with America's Limited Wars," *Washington Post,* October 9, 2014. Accessed March 5, 2016. https://www.washingtonpost.com/opinions/david-ignatius-reality-check-on-limited-war/2014/10/09/19c8c95e-4ff2-11e4-babe-e91da079cb8a_story.html.

97. Robert Michael Gates, *Duty: Memoirs of a Secretary at War* (New York: Knopf Doubleday Publishing, 2014), 383.

98. This can be well seen in the book *Fiasco*, by Tom Ricks.

99. Thomas Donnelly, "Rumsfeld's War," *Weekly Standard,* December 15, 2004, http://www.weeklystandard.com/rumsfelds-war/article/6246.

100. Strachan, *The Direction of War*, 45.

101. Clausewitz, *On War*, 75.

102. Photo credit: Wikipedia.

103. Photo credit: Horace Campbell.